But and For, Yet and Nor

Yet and Nor

What Is a Conjunction?

To Molly Hernan
—B.P.C.

Conjunction:
A word that joins together sentences, phrases, or words

All the conjunctions in this book that are given as examples are printed in color. A few additional conjunctions are not printed in color. For an extra challenge, see if you can spot them.

But and For, Yet and Nor

What Is a Conjunction?

by Brian P. Cleary

illustrations by Brian Gable

M... ...NEAPOLIS

Conjunctions
are connecting words

like but

or and

or or,

yet, until, unless, and as,

along with for and nor.

At times, conjunctions build a bridge

from one phrase to another, as in, "I picked some flowers

and gave them to my mother."

Other times,
conjunctions help
to link a pair of verbs,

Some will join two sentences,

combining them as one.

Like, "I could not be late to school,
So I began to run."

Or "When people meet him,

their faces all look sour,

12

because he can go
several days
without a bath
or shower."

Some think a conjunction

shouldn't ever be the word
that's used to start a sentence.

And why would I declare this?

So that everyone can see

GRAMMAR MYTHS

that sometimes a conjunction starts your sentence perfectly.

17

Some conjunctions work in pairs, like this one: either/or.

"We'll either eat our pizza on a plate

or off the floor."

Both and and and can work that way,
as in this next example:

both my parrot
and my friend

candy St

Tasting

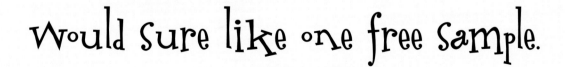

Would sure like one free sample.

Some have more to do with time,

like **after**
and **before**,

When and While,
until and Since,
to name a handful more.

23

See how these refer to "when"?

Like, "Since last May, I'm taller."

JUNE —
MAY —
APRIL —

Some conjunctions join

What doesn't seem

to go together.

Or "Mom's a ballroom dancing champ although she's quite a klutz."

Yes, all these are
connecting words—

no ifs,

no ands,

no buts!

So what is a conjunction?

Do you know?

Find activities, games, and more at
www.brianpcleary.com

ABOUT THE AUTHOR & ILLUSTRATOR

BRIAN P. CLEARY is the author of the best-selling Words Are CATegorical® series as well as the Math Is CATegorical®, Adventures in Memory™, and Sounds Like Reading® series. He is also the author of <u>The Punctuation Station</u>, <u>The Laugh Stand: Adventures in Humor</u>, <u>Peanut Butter and Jellyfishes: A Very Silly Alphabet Book</u>, and two poetry books. He lives in Cleveland, Ohio.

BRIAN GABLE is the illustrator of many Words Are CATegorical® books as well as the Math Is CATegorical® series. Mr. Gable also works as a political cartoonist for the *Globe and Mail* newspaper in Toronto, Canada, where he lives with his children.

Text copyright © 2010 by Brian P. Cleary
Illustrations copyright © 2010 by Lerner Publishing Group, Inc.

Millbrook Press
A division of Lerner Publishing Group, Inc.
241 First Avenue North
Minneapolis, MN 55401 U.S.A.

Website address: www.lernerbooks.com

Library of Congress Cataloging-in-Publication Data

Cleary, Brian P., 1959-
　　But and for, yet and nor : what is a conjunction? / by Brian P. Cleary ; illustrated by Brian Gable.
　　　　p.　　cm. — (Words are CATegorical)
　　ISBN: 978-0-8225-9153-5 (lib. bdg. : alk. paper)
　　1. English language—Conjunctions—Juvenile literature. I. Gable, Brian, 1949- ill. II. Title.
　PE1345.C54　2010
　425—dc22　　　　　　　　　　　　　　　　　　　　　　　　　　　　2009015861

Manufactured in the United States of America
1 — JR — 12/15/09